HOW TO RAISE AND TRAIN A BORZOI

A brace of red and white Champion Borzois, Ch. Sascha Kochab of Hethivar, C.D.X., and his litter sister, Ch. Shahzana Kochab of Hethivar, C.D., both owned by Charles and Gail McRae.

By Gail McRae

Distributed in the U.S.A. by T.F.H. Publications, Inc., 211 West Sylvania Avenue, P.O. Box 27, Neptune City, N.J. 07753; in England by T.F.H. (Gt. Britain) Ltd., 13 Nutley Lane, Reigate, Surrey; in Canada to the book store and library trade by Clarke, Irwin & Company, Clarwin House, 791 St. Clair Avenue West, Toronto 10, Ontario; in Canada to the pet trade by Rolf C. Hagen Ltd., 3225 Sartelon Street, Montreal 382, Quebec; in Southeast Asia by Y.W. Ong, 9 Lorong 36 Geylang, Singapore 14; in Australia and the south Pacific by Pet Imports Pty. Ltd., P.O. Box 149, Brookvale 2100, N.S.W., Australia. Published by T.F.H. Publications Inc. Ltd., The British Crown Colony of Hong Kong.

Cover illustration: International Champion Yer-
maks Rurick holds the Dog World Award of
Canine Distinction. Owned by Marge and Sid
Cox. Photo by Louise Van der Meid.

ISBN 0-87666-250-5

Contents

1. Character and History

This noble, ancient breed called Borzoi (or Russian Wolfhound) is the aristocrat of the canine world. He is considered by many the most beautiful and intelligent of the "sight hounds." The term "sight hound" applies to the coursing hounds, or hounds which depend on their keen vision for sighting game at great distances. Borzois are known for their speed and agility in overtaking such quarry as the wolf, hare, fox, and coyote.

APPEARANCE

Resembling Greyhounds in general appearance, Borzois are slightly taller and more muscular with a long coat. Their bearing conveys the impression of being swift, capable hunters and, at the same time, gentle, well-behaved pets.

Ch. Yermaks Rurick, holder of the **Dog World** award of Canine Distinction. Owners: Marge and Sid Cox. Photo by Joan Ludwig.

As they are one of the tallest recognized breeds in the world, it is not unusual to see Borzois reaching 36 inches high at the withers. Their appearance is quite elegant, possessing lines that suggest both fleetness and great muscular power.

Their coats are most impressive, being long and wavy or curly with a very silky texture. Any color is acceptable, the most common colors being white or cream with red, black, gold, or gray markings. Occasionally whole-colored specimens appear in pure black or red with white trim on neck, chest, and tail. It was customary in Russia for a gentleman's "leash" (three dogs) to be white, hence the popular notion that Borzois should be white.

Large in size, Borzois are nevertheless gentle, trustworthy, and most contented when treated as members of the family. Borzois are very possessive and protective of home and family and jealously guard those they love. They need and seek the affection of the family and are well known for their gentleness with children.

The Borzoi head is long and narrow with oblique, soft, and expressive eyes. The ears are small, lying back on the neck with the tips almost touching. When alerted, the ears are raised and, in puppies, are carried in an assortment

Four-months-old Borzoi puppies combine natural puppy charm with an old and proud heritage. Borzois owned by Tam-Boer Kennels.

This is an interesting head study of Ch. Perchinoff Ciadona O'Zcerlov, whose full body portrait appears elswhere in this book. She is owned by J. Andre Legere.

of positions, sometimes straight up or sometimes with one over the top of the head. This is called making "bonnets" with their ears, and as soon as the puppy has completed the teething process, the ears will be carried in the correct position.

The neck is powerful and slightly arched. The chest is rather narrow, but the brisket is very deep with only slightly sprung ribs, never barrel-shaped or too slab-sided. The back rises gently in a graceful arch with the loins well tucked up, allowing room for free action of the hind legs in quick turns. The hindquarters are very muscular and powerful with well-bent stifles.

The tail is set low and carried in a low graceful curve. When hunting or running, the tail is carried higher and acts as a balance on sharp turns, but it should not be carried higher than the level of the back and should not curl tightly at the end.

Because the Borzoi develops slowly and is seldom mature until the age of three and sometimes four years, young dogs should not be expected to have the depth of brisket called for in the standard until such an age is reached.

The feet of the Borzoi are hare-shaped with well-arched knuckles.

Although the standard makes no particular mention of gait, one must keep in mind that the Borzoi is an active hunting dog, depending on his speed and coordination to catch his quarry. A good Borzoi, well put together, will have a light flowing gait with a good reach in front when trotting. The gait should not be short and choppy. The feet should not turn in or out, nor should the front feet cross over each other when the dog is gaiting (a condition known as weaving). The hindquarters, which must express strength, are wider than the front quarters, giving great stability.

DISPOSITION

When it comes to disposition the Borzoi is Marvelous, with a capital "M." He seems to understand everything said to him and loves most of all to be close to his master. He has a unique way of greeting you, by actually smiling: he will wrinkle his nose and show his teeth when he is very happy. He gets along very well with other Borzois, even forming close attachments. Most Borzois are seen in braces of two and are commonly pictured two together. Usually, if you have one Borzoi, you like it so well, you want a second. Therefore, most people have two or more Borzois, if space permits. However, it is not necessary to keep more than one; with love and attention, a Borzoi is quite happy to be in a one-dog family. The prospective buyer, seeking a pet, may have doubts about purchasing a dog that has been bred to hunt wolves. But even Borzois that have the opportunity to hunt are most gentle animals.

A striking black Borzoi, Ch. Trezor Briansk, owned by Russell O. Everhart. This dog was sired by Ch. Winjones Janda; dam: Ramadan Koraleva Chevry.

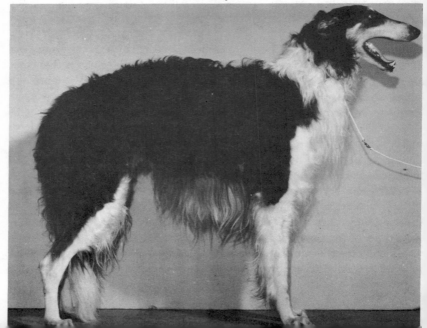

This is the well-known West Coast winner, Ch. Hollister of Rancho Gabriel. Sire: Ch. Solentse of Alpine, C.D.; Dam: Aida of Rancho Gabriel. Bred, owned, and handled by Phydelma and Lyle E. Gillette. Photo by Photo Annex.

HISTORY

Coursing hounds are known to have existed for many centuries. This is evidenced by drawings in ancient tombs and on monuments in Egypt, depicting scenes of dogs closely resembling our modern-day sight hounds. Coursing originally was not a sport but a matter of necessity. The hounds were depended upon as a means of procuring food for survival. As man progressed, his dependence upon the hounds grew less and less. Coursing however, did not cease as a result of this progress, but became popular as sport among kings.

The exact origin and history of the Borzoi is not entirely agreed upon by authorities and writings on the breed. From the records that are known, the first standard was established in 1650 and closely resembles the present-day standard. The Borzoi was developed by crossing two of the most ancient types of Russian Windhounds. One of these was large and quite beautiful and excellent for coursing hares. The other, more powerful, and with a curly coat, was used for coursing wolves and wild boars. From these two hounds developed the original Borzoi.

The favorite sport of seventeenth century Russian nobility was coursing or hunting deer, foxes, hares, and wolves. The wolf was considered the most prized catch, and the hounds used on this quarry had to be swift, powerful and courageous. One of the most ardent and well known of the Russian nobility to maintain vast kennels of Borzois was The Grand Duke Nikolai Nikolaivitch, who in 1887 purchased the famous Perchina Estate and founded one of the most renowned breed lines, the Perchina Borzois.

The Grand Duke maintained as many as 150 to 160 Borzois in his kennels at one time. When hunting, the dogs went together three on a leash, matched in size and color, two dogs and one bitch. When the quarry was sighted, the

This photograph well illustrates the photogenic qualities of the Borzoi. Lovely screen star Rhonda Fleming poses with Ch. Lady of Bolshoi and Ch. Rubles Perchino, owned by Mr. and Mrs. Charles N. Colstad.

Bourtai of Malora, the first American and Canadian U.D. Borzoi, poses proudly among the impressive array of trophies he has won. This fine Borzoi is owned, trained, and handled by Gordon Sohr.

hounds were released to give chase. Two of the trio would overtake the wolf and pin him to the ground by securing a firm grip behind the wolf's ears with their powerful jaws. The third Borzoi would hold the wolf by the throat until the hunter on horseback rode up and pinioned the wolf. The best wolves caught in this manner were kept for training the young hounds in the art of the chase. Because of their extreme swiftness, agility, courage, and ability to sight, catch, and hold their prey, these hounds were a highly cherished possession. It was considered disgraceful to sell Borzois, but they were occasionally presented as gifts to other members of the nobility. Nicholas II of Russia made such a presentation to England's Princess of Wales (later Queen Alexandra) in 1895.

As early as 1860, British royalty, including the Prince of Wales and the Duchess of Newcastle, bred and exhibited Borzois that had been presented to them by Russian nobility. The first Borzoi exhibited at a British dog show (1863) was "Sultan," who was the property of the Duchess of Manchester. He was bred by Prince Charles of Prussia. After the Russian Revolution, the large estates and kennels were forced to abandon their beautiful hounds, and many of them found their way to England and other European countries.

In 1892 the Borzoi Club of England was founded. Among the early promoters of the breed in England was Col. and Mrs. Wellesley. They were presented with a dog named "Krillutt" by the Czar while Col. Wellesley was attached to the British Embassy in Russia. The exhibiting of the Wellesley dogs in London helped establish the Borzoi vogue that followed in England, Canada, and the United States.

In 1890, William Wade, of Hulton, imported the first Borzois to the United States. Later, in the early 1890's, Stedman Hanks, of Boston, imported several of the breed directly from Russia, as did Joseph B. Thomas, whose hounds came from the famous Perchina and Woronzova kennels. In 1893, the American Kennel Club had a total registration of eight Russian Wolfhounds. Several enthusiastic breeders formed a club in 1903 known as the Russian Wolfhound Club of America. This club developed a standard of quality and perfection used by all the breeders, judges, and show committees of the early 1900's. In 1936, the breed name was officially changed to "Borzoi," making it conform with the name used by European kennel clubs.

Can there be any question that a Borzoi is built for speed? Ch. Sunbarr's Bengal Lancer gives the impression of swiftness, even when standing in a show ring. Photo by Benyas-Kaufman Photographers.

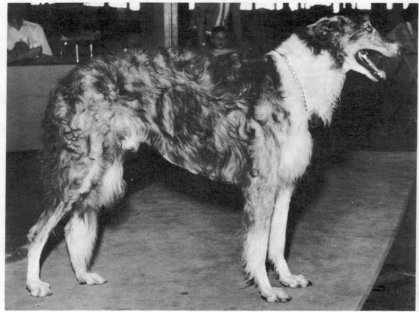

Three lovelies. The young lady poses with two champions of the Warhill Kennels. At the left is Ch. Trezor Donitz of Warhill and at the right Ch. Warhill's Amber Roi.

Borzois were very popular in the "Roaring Twenties." They were the proud possessions of many movie celebrities and appeared in some of Ziegfeld's famous productions. Their use in high-style fashion photography, modeling, movies, and television is prominent to this day. The breed is still relatively rare, although their popularity is showing an upward trend in recent years as more and more dog lovers are becoming familiar with this versatile and lovable dog.

USES

Through the centuries, the Borzois' inherent hunting instincts and abilities have remained with them. Without formal training they will readily chase and capture game. Because of this natural ability Borzois are highly valued by ranchers throughout the United States and Canada for the hunting of coyotes. A single Borzoi is easily capable of overtaking and killing a coyote.

Borzois are also used extensively in the United States and England as show dogs, always creating a great attraction for spectators wherever they appear. They are always among the quietest, most dignified and relaxed of the dogs to be seen at a show. The Borzois' ability in obedience trials has

This is the famous winner Ch. Ducies Wild of Tam-Boer. He was sired by Ch. Dutchie of Tam-Boer; dam: Ch. Little Joker of Tam-Boer. Ducies' fine record of breed wins include some of the most important shows in the country. He is owned by the Tam-Boer Kennels. Photo by Rudolph Tauskey.

Ch. Dutchie of Tam-Boer, the distinguished sire of such fine Borzois as Ch. Ducies Wild and Kiki of Tam-Boer.

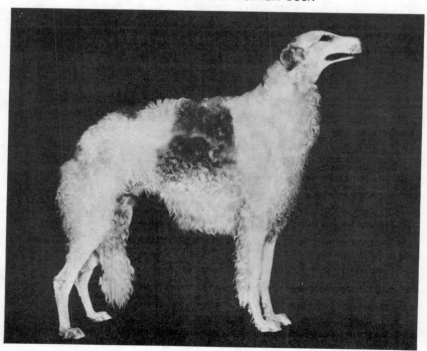

Ch. Loral's Alpha Nicholai. This photograph shows the classic unspoiled elegance of the true running hound. This handsome fawn and white male was sired by Ch. Nicholas Siberius; dam: Arlekeen of Frontier. He was bred and is owned by Mrs. Albert Groshans. Photo by Kenneth Clauser.

helped educate the public to realize that this animal is not only a thing of beauty but also is highly intelligent as well. In Russia today, the Borzoi is still valued as a hunter. He is required to show a certificate attesting to his hunting abilities prior to being accepted for showing.

BORZOI STANDARD

HEAD—Skull slightly domed, long and narrow, with scarcely any perceptible stop, rather inclined to be Roman-nosed; jaws long, powerful, and deep; teeth strong, clean, and even, neither pig-jawed nor undershot; nose large and black.

EARS—Small and fine in quality, lying back on the neck when in repose, with the tips when thrown back almost touching behind occiput; raised when at attention.

EYES—Set somewhat obliquely, dark in color, intelligent, but rather soft in expression, never full nor staring, nor light in color; eyelids dark.

NECK—Clean, free from throatiness, somewhat shorter than in the Greyhound, slightly arched, very powerful, and well set on.

SHOULDERS—Sloping, should be fine at the withers and free from coarseness or lumber.

CHEST—Rather narrow, with great depth of brisket.

RIBS—Only slightly sprung but very deep, giving room for heart and lung play.

BACK—Rising a little at the loins in a graceful curve.

LOINS—Extremely muscular, but rather tucked up, owing to the great depth of chest and comparative shortness of back and ribs.

FORELEGS—Bone flat, straight, giving free play for the elbows, which should be neither turned in nor out; pasterns strong.

FEET—Hare-shaped, with well-arched knuckles, toes close and well padded.

HINDQUARTERS—Long, very muscular and powerful, with well-bent stifles and strong second thighs; hocks broad, clean, and well let down.

TAIL—Long, set on and carried low in a graceful curve.

COAT—Long, silky (not woolly), either flat, wavy, or rather curly. On the head, ears, and front of legs, it should be short and smooth; on the neck, the frill should be profuse and rather curly. Feather on hindquarters and tail, long and profuse, less so on the chest and back of forelegs.

COLOR—Any color, white usually predominating, more or less marked with lemon, tan, brindle, grey, or black. Whole-colored specimens of these tints occasionally appear.

GENERAL APPEARANCE—Should be that of an elegant, graceful aristocrat among dogs, possessing courage and combining muscular power with extreme speed.

SIZE—Dogs, average height at withers from 28 to 31 inches; average weight from 75 to 105 pounds. Larger dogs are often seen, extra size being no disadvantage when it is not acquired at the expense of symmetry, speed, and staying quality. Bitches are invariably smaller than dogs; two inches less in height and from 15 to 20 pounds less in weight is a fair average.

	Points
Head	12
Eyes	5
Ears	3
Neck	5
Shoulders and brisket	10
Ribs, back and loins	15
Hindquarters, stifles and hocks	12
Legs and feet	10
Coat and feather	10
Tail	3
Conformation and gait	15
Total	100

The address of the American Kennel Club is 51 Madison Avenue, New York, N.Y. 10010.

Ch. Yermaks Ekatrina, owned by Genevieve Pitcock, shows a beautiful Borzoi head. Photo by Johansen Studio.

A head study of Ch. Shahzana Kochab of Hethivar, C.D., showing the typical alert Borzoi expression. She is owned by Charles and Gail McRae.

Ch. Tersai of Gwejon. This fine male has won the **Dog World** award as an outstanding winner. Bred, owned, and handled by Mr. and Mrs. John M. Pinnette.

17

2. Environment Suitable To The Breed

EXERCISE

It is not necessary to have a ranch to provide Borzois with a happy home. They are easily adapted to the smaller quarters available to the average city home-owner. Exercise is an important need of the breed, as Borzois were bred to run and should be given regular exercise to develop and maintain good condition. There are almost always large open areas available to city dwellers in the form of parks, recreational areas, and beaches. Take your Borzoi out and give him a good run regularly. In the event these areas are not available or convenient, a daily walk with your dog should be practiced.

THE ADULT'S DIET

In order to maintain a happy and healthy pet, proper diet is essential. The Borzoi's appetite is easily catered to, as he is not a large eater. In most

Ch. Czaru of Twin Elms, a hound group winner, was sired by Ch. Zabu of Twin Elms, C.D.; dam: Malora's Talisman of Twin Elms. Owned, bred, and handled by Gordon Sohr. Photo by Frasie Studios.

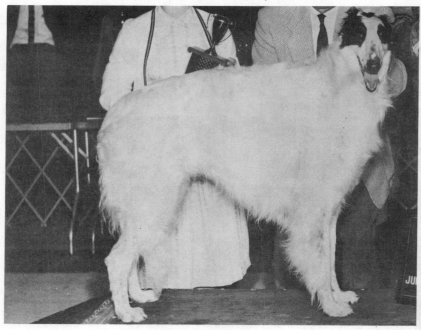

Ch. Czarina HHF of Gwejon, Amer. and Can. C.D.X. Czarina is the only Borzoi Champion to hold the title of C.D.X. in the United States and Canada. She is owned by Mr. and Mrs. John M. Pinette, and is shown in this picture with Mr. Pinette.

Ch. Alta of Alpine. This lovely Borzoi finished her championship at twenty months of age. Photo by Joan Ludwig.

cases an adult Borzoi may be kept in fit condition with one meal a day. Usually the best results are achieved by feeding a good kibble mixed with at least one pound of cooked or raw beef. When using cooked meat, be sure that the food has cooled to room temperature before feeding.

Extreme care should be exercised in feeding bones. Under no circumstances give him a bone from fowl, as these hollow bones splinter easily and may puncture or cause a blockage in the digestive tract. If a bone is given at all, it should be a large knuckle bone. Rawhide and nylon bones make excellent substitutes for real bones.

The regular addition of fat in the form of bacon fat or lard is recommended to keep the Borzoi's skin and coat in excellent condition. Table scraps other than meat are not recommended at any time, because a dog's digestive system is not adapted to digesting the foods eaten by human beings. Be sure your dog's mealtime, like your own, is on a regular schedule. Most petshops offer a good selection of foods for you to choose for your pet's diet.

Puppy diet is covered in chapter four.

SHELTER

The Borzoi is a hardy dog that can endure and enjoy very cold weather, but he requires a sheltered area that will afford him some comfort and protection from drafts during his relaxing or sleeping periods. If you plan to

Ch. Bolshoi of Baronoff, sired by Ch. Rachmaninoff; dam, Ch. Sascha of Baronoff. Bred and owned by Mr. and Mrs. Weldon J. McCluskey. Photo by Evelyn Shafer.

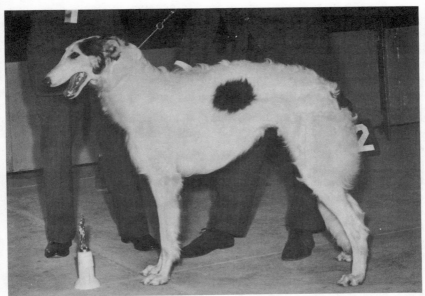

Ch. Trezor Donitz of Warhill. Sire: Ch. Jaguar Jehan of Malora; dam: Ramadan Koraleva Chevry. This fine Borzoi is owned by the Warhill Kennels. Photo by Frasie Studios.

This group-winning Borzoi is Ch. Tamazar of Twin Elms, bred, owned, and handled by Gordon Sohr. Photo by Frasie Studios.

kennel your Borzoi outdoors, his shelter must be built off the ground with a doorway that is not exposed directly to the wind. This will protect him against drafts that may cause colds. The size of the shelter should provide enough room for him to stand and move about freely. It should include some ventilation for summer heat and, if possible, be situated in a shaded area. To provide some comfort for your pet, straw, blankets, or rugs may be used as bedding in the shelter.

As mentioned earlier, the Borzoi makes an ideal house pet, so if you prefer, he may be kept indoors; he is an extremely clean and well-behaved animal.

COLLARS AND LEADS

Your Borzoi will require a metal slip chain collar and a leather leash, the latter being at least six feet long. Leather collars and shoulder harnesses should not be used, as they tend to rub the hair off, and you have less control over the dog with this type of equipment. Treat your Borzoi as one of the family, care for him with common sense and you will enjoy many years of wonderful companionship with him.

These five Rancho Gabriel Borzois prove how well they get along together.

3. Grooming

BRUSHING

Your Borzoi puppy will grow very rapidly, so it is best to start good grooming practices at an early age. The Borzoi does not require extensive grooming to maintain a clean, shiny coat. A daily brushing and combing should be practiced to remove loose dirt and tangles. To brush his coat you should use a medium-length bristle brush that is not too stiff. A stiff-bristled brush will break and tear out the hair. When brushing the hair on the back and the neck, brush it forward towards the head. Brush the rest of the coat in the usual manner, in the direction the hair grows. A ten-minute brushing daily will reduce the need for frequent bathing, which is not generally beneficial to a dog.

Marbob's Romulus of Malora strikes a perfect show pose, unassisted. This dog is owned by Charlotte Wheeler. Photo by January.

BATHING

If an occasional bath is given, such as in preparation for a dog show, take care to bathe your dog in an area where he will not become chilled. The best method is to use an ordinary bathtub and a hose spray. Before you begin, place a little piece of cotton in each of the dog's ears and a drop of mineral oil in each eye to prevent accidental entry of irritating substances. Start by wetting the dog's coat from the neck back to the tail. Use a dog shampoo, of which there are several types; human shampoos are not recommended. Lather the dog all over and then rinse all traces of shampoo from the coat. Do the head last, as most dogs object to a wet head. When the bath is finished, dry your dog quickly and briskly with some good-size bath towels. Be careful not to allow your dog to become chilled, as he is as susceptible to catching colds as you are. If the weather is fair and sunny it is advisable to take him for a walk. This will keep his circulation going and help to dry him more quickly.

CARE OF THE FEET

The care of the dog's feet is very important and must not be neglected. Long claws will spread the toes and cause a "splayed-foot" condition, or if left to grow too long will result in ingrown claws which will cause him a great deal of discomfort. A regularly exercised dog will have little trouble with his

This lovely all-white Borzoi is Ch. Perchinoff Ciadona O'Zcerlov, owned by J. Andre Legere and handled by Dorothea Metzger. Photo by Joan Ludwig.

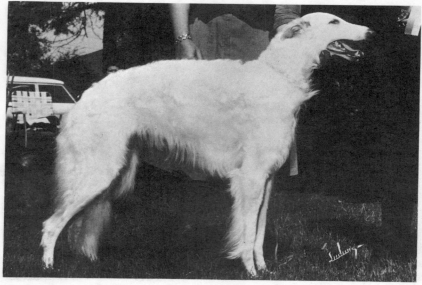

Ch. Mythe Marova of Alpine, shown winning Best of Opposite Sex at the
Borzoi Club of California specialty.

This magnificent West Coast Borzoi winner is Ch. Talix of Twin Elms,
owned by Edw. Stepnoski. Photo by Bennett Associates.

feet, as exercising on concrete will keep the claws worn short. If you plan to hunt with your dog, inspect his pads to be sure they are not cracking or becoming worn too thin.

The dewclaw is really a fifth toe appearing on the inner side of the leg and should be removed a few days after birth of the puppy. Dewclaws detract from the appearance of the dog and can possibly be torn off later in life if the dog runs through rough country or even catches it on a fence. If they are left on, it will be necessary to cut them even more frequently than the other claws, because they do not touch the ground and therefore do not get the wear necessary to keep them short.

Borzois come in many interesting color combinations. This one is a tricolor, Ch. Geroi of Grador, owned by John F. Goring, Jr. Photo by Joan Ludwig.

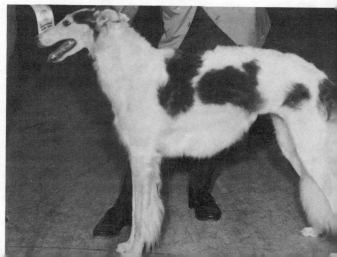

Ch. Natasha of Shore Acres. Sire: Ch. Boi of Rolling Meadows; dam: Dedlova of Mettler Hobby Farm, owned by Warhill Kennels. Photo by Frasie Studios.

Five Borzois, all from the same litter, sired by Ch. Walzoff Perchinoff; dam: Zcerlov's Zoltka. They are from left to right Ch. Perchinoff Rubles O'Zcerlov, Perchinoff Zinaida O'Zcerlov, Ch. Perchinoff Gorki O'Zcerlov, Ch. Perchinoff Ciadona O'Zcerlov, and Perchinoff Zagor O'Zcerlov. Photo by Norman.

The outside area your Borzoi has access to should not be completely smooth, such as all concrete. A rough ground cover such as pea sized gravel is good to keep the feet from becoming too flat or splayed.

Because neglect of eyes, ears, teeth, and claws can lead to health problems, the care of these body parts is discussed in chapter eight, Health.

CLIPPING AND SHOW PREPARATION

Your Borzoi will require no clipping in the sense that a Poodle or Cocker does. His appearance is natural and unaltered. In preparing him for a dog show, and in order to give him a well-groomed appearance, it is suggested that his whiskers be trimmed off. Trim the excess hair that protrudes from the ears, as it will tend to make the skull look wider. The excess hair between the toes should be taken off to give the feet a neater appearance. A pair of barber scissors and thinning shears are all that is required for these preparations. Until you become familiar with handling both, take it easy when trimming your Borzoi. It is better to take off too little than too much. Remember to trim the dog at least two weeks before the show.

The night before the show, bathe the dog and brush him well and you will be all set to go.

4. The New Puppy

PREPARING FOR THE PUPPY'S ARRIVAL

Because at least three out of four prospective purchasers of dogs want to buy a young rather than an adult or almost adult dog, the problem of preparing for the arrival of a permanent canine house guest almost always means preparing for the arrival of a puppy. This is not to say that there is anything wrong with purchasing an adult dog; on the contrary, such a purchase has definite advantages in that it often allows freedom from housebreaking chores and rigorous feeding schedules, and these are of definite benefit to prospective purchasers who have little time to spare. Since the great majority of dog buyers, however, prefer to watch their pet grow from sprawlingly playful puppyhood to dignified maturity, buying a dog, practically speaking, means buying a puppy.

Before you get a puppy be sure that you are willing to take the responsibility of training him and caring for his physical needs. His early training is most important, as an adult dog that is a well-behaved member of the family is the end product of your early training. Remember that your new puppy knows only a life of romping with his littermates and the security of being with his mother, and that coming into your home is a new and sometimes frightening experience for him. He will adjust quickly if you are patient with him and show him what you expect of him. If there are small children in the family be sure that they do not abuse him or play roughly with him. A puppy plays hard, but he also requires frequent periods of rest. Before he comes, decide where he is to sleep and where he is to eat. If your puppy does not have a collar, find out the size he requires and buy an inexpensive one, as he will soon outgrow it. Have the proper grooming equipment on hand. Consult the person from whom you bought the puppy as to the proper food for your puppy, and learn the feeding time and amount that he eats a day. Buy him some toys—usually the breeder will give you some particular toy or toys which he has cherished as a puppy to add to his new ones and to make him less homesick. Get everything you need from your petshop *before* you bring the puppy home.

MALE OR FEMALE?

Before buying your puppy you should have made a decision as to whether you want a male or a female. Unless you want to breed your pet and raise a litter of puppies, your preference as to the sex of your puppy is strictly a personal choice. Both sexes are pretty much the same in disposition and character, and both make equally good pets.

WHERE TO BUY YOUR PUPPY

Although petshop owners are necessarily restricted from carrying all breeds in stock, they know the best dog breeders and are sometimes able to supply quality puppies on demand. In cases in which a petshop owner is unable to obtain a dog for you, he can still refer you to a good source, such as a reputable kennel. If your local petshop proprietor is unable to either obtain a dog for you or refer you to someone from whom you can purchase one, don't give up: there are other avenues to explore. The American Kennel Club will furnish you addresses. Additional sources of information are the various magazines devoted to the dog fancy.

SIGNS OF GOOD HEALTH

Picking out a healthy, attractive little fellow to join the family circle is a different matter from picking a show dog; it is also a great deal less complicated. Often the puppy will pick you. If he does, and it is mutual admiration at first sight, he is the best puppy for you. At a reliable kennel or petshop the owner will be glad to answer your questions and to point out the difference between pet and show-quality puppies. Trust your eyes and hands to tell if the puppies are sound in body and temperament. Ears and eyes should not have suspicious discharges. Legs should have strong bones; bodies should have solid muscles. Coats should be clean. Lift the hair to see if the skin is free of scales and parasites.

Temperament can vary from puppy to puppy in the same litter. There is always one puppy which will impress you by his energy and personality. He loves to show off and will fling himself all over you and his littermates, and everyone who comes to see the puppies falls in love with him. However, do not overlook the more reserved puppy. Most dogs are wary of strangers, so reserve may indicate caution, not a timid puppy. He may calmly accept your presence when he senses that all is well. Such a puppy should be a steady reliable dog when mature. In any event, never force yourself on a puppy — let him come to you. Reliable breeders and petshops will urge you to take your puppy to the veterinarian of your choice to have the puppy's health checked, and will allow you at least two days in which to have it done. It should be clearly understood whether rejection by a veterinarian for health reasons means that you have the choice of another puppy from that litter or that you get your money back.

AGE AT WHICH PUPPY SHOULD BE PURCHASED

A puppy should be at least six weeks of age before you take him home. Many breeders will not let puppies go before they are two months old. In general, the puppy you buy for show and breeding should be five or six months old. If you want a show dog, remember that not even an expert can predict with 100% accuracy what a small puppy will be when he grows up.

PAPERS

When you buy a purebred dog you should receive his American Kennel Club registration certificate (or an application form to fill out), a pedigree, and a health certificate made out by the breeder's veterinarian. The registration certificate is the official A.K.C. paper. If the puppy was named and registered by his breeder you will want to complete the transfer and send it, with the fee, to the American Kennel Club. They will transfer the dog to your ownership in their records and send a new certificate to you. If you receive, instead, an application for registration, you should fill it out, choosing a name for your dog, and mail it, with the fee, to the A.K.C.

The pedigree is a chart showing your puppy's ancestry and is not a part of his official papers. The health certificate will tell what shots have been given and when the next ones are due. Your veterinarian will be appreciative of this information, and will continue with the same series of shots if they have not been completed. The health certificate will also give the dates on which the puppy has been wormed. Ask your veterinarian whether rabies shots are required in your locality. Most breeders will give you food for a few days along with instructions for feeding so that your puppy will have the same diet he is accustomed to until you can buy a supply at your petshop.

THE PUPPY'S FIRST NIGHT WITH YOU

The puppy's first night at home is likely to be disturbing to the family. Keep in mind that suddenly being away from his mother, brothers, and sisters is a new experience for him; he may be confused and frightened. If you have a special room in which you have his bed, be sure that there is nothing there with which he can harm himself. Be sure that all lamp cords are out of his reach and that there is nothing that he can tip or pull over. Check furniture that he might get stuck under or behind and objects that he might chew. If you want him to sleep in your room he probably will be quiet all night, reassured by your presence. If left in a room by himself he will cry and howl, and you will have to steel yourself to be impervious to his whining. After a few nights alone he will adjust. The first night that he is alone it is wise to put a loud-ticking alarm clock, as well as his toys, in the room with him. The alarm clock will make a comforting noise, and he will not feel that he is alone.

YOUR PUPPY'S BED

Every dog likes to have a place that is his alone. He holds nothing more sacred than his own bed whether it be a rug, dog crate, or dog bed. If you get your puppy a bed be sure to get one which discourages chewing. Also be sure that the bed is large enough to be comfortable for him when he is fully grown. Locate it away from drafts and radiators. A word might be said here in defense of the crate, which many pet owners think is cruel and confining. Given a choice, a young dog instinctively selects a secure place

Special dog feeding and watering utensils are so designed as to safe-guard your pet from dangerous porcelain chips. These utensils are easy to keep clean, too.

in which to lounge, rest, or sleep. The walls and ceiling of a crate, even a wire one, answer that need. Once he regards his crate as a safe and reassuring place to stay, you will be able to leave him alone in the house.

FEEDING YOUR PUPPY

As a general rule, a puppy from weaning time (six weeks) to three months of age should have *four meals a day;* from three months to six months, *three meals;* from six months to one year, *two meals.* After a year, a dog does well on *one meal daily.* There are as many feeding schedules as there are breeders, and puppies do fine on all of them, so it is best for the new owner to follow the one given him by the breeder of his puppy. Remember that all dogs are individuals. The amount that will keep your dog in good health is right for him, not the "rule-book" amount. A feeding schedule to give you some idea of what the average puppy will eat is as follows:

Morning meal: Puppy meal with milk.
Afternoon meal: Meat mixed with puppy meal, plus a vitamin-mineral supplement.
Evening meal: Same as afternoon meal, but without a vitamin-mineral supplement.

Do not change the amounts in your puppy's diet too rapidly. If he gets diarrhea it may be that he is eating too much, so cut back on his food and when he is normal again increase his food more slowly.

There is a canned food made especially for puppies which you can buy only by a veterinarian's prescription. Some breeders use this very successfully from weaning to three months.

TRANSITIONAL DIET

Changing over to an adult program of feeding is not difficult. Very often the puppy will change himself; that is, he will refuse to eat some of his meals. He adjusts to his one meal (or two meals) a day without any trouble at all.

BREAKING TO COLLAR AND LEASH

Puppies are usually broken to a collar before you bring them home, but even if yours has never worn one it is a simple matter to get him used to it. Put a loose collar on him for a few hours at a time. At first he may scratch at it and try to get it off, but gradually he will take it as a matter of course. To break him to a lead, attach his leash to his collar and let him drag it around. When he becomes used to it pick it up and gently pull him in the direction you want him to go. He will think it is a game, and with a bit of patience on your part he will allow himself to be led.

DISCIPLINING YOUR PUPPY

The way to have a well-mannered adult dog is to give him firm basic training while he is a puppy. When you say *"No"* you must mean *"No."* Your dog will respect you only if you are firm. A six- to eight-weeks-old puppy is old enough to understand what *"No"* means. The first time you see your puppy doing something he shouldn't be doing, chewing something he shouldn't chew, or wandering in a forbidden area, it's time to teach him. Shout, *"No."* Puppies do not like loud noises, and your misbehaving pet will readily connect the word with something unpleasant. Usually a firm *"No"* in a disapproving tone of voice is enough to correct your dog, but occasionally you get a puppy that requires a firmer hand, especially as he grows older. In this case hold your puppy firmly and slap him gently across the hindquarters. If this seems cruel, you should realize that no dog resents being disciplined if he is caught in the act of doing something wrong, and your puppy will be intelligent enough to know what the slap was for.

After you have slapped him and you can see that he has learned his lesson, call him to you and talk to him in a pleasant tone of voice — praise him for coming to you. This sounds contradictory, but it works with a puppy. He immediately forgives you, practically tells you that it was his fault and that he deserved his punishment, and promises that it will not happen again. This form of discipline works best and may be used for all misbehaviors.

Never punish your puppy by chasing him around, making occasional swipes with a rolled-up newspaper; punish him only when you have a firm hold on him. Above all, never punish your dog after having called him to you. He must learn to associate coming to you with something pleasant.

HOUSEBREAKING

While housebreaking your puppy do not let him have the run of the house. If you do you will find that he will pick out his own bathroom, which may be in your bedroom or in the middle of the living room rug. Keep him confined to a small area where you can watch him, and you will be able to train him much more easily and speedily. A puppy does not want to dirty his bed, but he does need to be taught where he should go. Spread papers over his living quarters, then watch him carefully. When you notice him starting to whimper, sniff the floor, or run agitatedly in little circles, rush him to the place that you want to serve as his relief area and gently hold him there until he relieves himself. Then praise him lavishly. When you remove the soiled papers, leave a small damp piece so that the puppy's sense of smell will lead him back there next time. If he makes a mistake, wash the area at once with warm water, followed by a rinse with water and vinegar or sudsy ammonia. This will kill the odor and prevent discoloration. It shouldn't take more than a few days for him to get the idea of using newspapers. When he becomes fairly consistent, reduce the area of paper to a few sheets in a corner. As soon as you think he has the idea fixed in his mind, you can let him roam around the house a bit, but keep an eye on him. It might be best to keep him on leash the first few days so that you can rush him back to his paper at any signs of an approaching accident.

The normal healthy puppy will want to relieve himself when he wakes in the morning, after each feeding, and after strenuous exercise. During early puppyhood any excitement, such as the return home of a member of the family or the approach of a visitor, may result in floor-wetting, but that phase should pass in a few weeks. Keep in mind that you can't expect too much from your puppy until he is about five months old. Before that, his muscles and digestive system just aren't under his control.

OUTDOOR HOUSEBREAKING

You can begin outdoor training on leash even while you are paper-training your puppy. First thing in the morning take him outdoors (to the curb, if you are in the city) and walk him back and forth in a small area until he relieves himself. He will probably make a puddle and then walk around, uncertain of what is expected of him. You can try standing him over a newspaper, which may give him the idea. Some dog trainers use glycerine suppositories at this point for fast action. Praise your dog every time taking him outside brings results, and he will get the idea. You'll find, when you begin the outdoor training, that the male puppy usually requires a longer walk than the female. Both male and female puppies will squat. It isn't until he is older that the male dog will begin to lift his leg. If you hate to give up your sleep, you can train your puppy to go outdoors during the day and use the paper at night.

5. Training

WHEN TO START TRAINING

You should never begin SERIOUS obedience training before your d
is seven or eight months old. (Some animal psychologists state that puppi
can begin training when seven weeks old, if certain techniques are followe
These techniques, however, are still experimental and should be left to tl
professional trainer to prove their worth.) While your dog is still in his ear
puppyhood, concentrate on winning his confidence so he will love ar
admire you. This will make his training easier, since he will do anythi
to please you. Basic training can be started at the age of three or fo
months. He should be taught to walk nicely on a leash, sit and lie down
command, and come when he is called.

YOUR PART IN TRAINING

You must patiently demonstrate to your dog what each word of commar
means. Guide him with your hands and the training leash, reassuring hi
with your voice, through whatever routine you are teaching him. Repeat tl
word associated with the act. Demonstrate again and again to give the d
a chance to make the connection in his mind.

Once he begins to get the idea, use the word of command without ar
physical guidance. Drill him. When he makes mistakes, correct him, kind
at first, more severely as his training progresses. Try not to lose yo
patience or become irritated, and never slap him with your hand or tl
leash during the training session. Withholding praise or rebuking him w
make him feel bad enough.

When he does what you want, praise him lavishly with words and wi
pats. Don't continually reward with dog candy or treats in training. Tl
dog that gets into the habit of performing for a treat will seldom be ful
dependable when he can't smell or see one in the offing. When he carri
out a command, even though his performance is slow or sloppy, praise hi
and he will perform more readily the next time.

THE TRAINING VOICE

When you start training your dog, use your training voice, giving con
mands in a firm, clear tone. Once you give a command, persist until it
obeyed, even if you have to pull the dog to obey you. He must learn th
training is different from playing, that a command once given must l
obeyed no matter what distractions are present. Remember that the to
and pitch of your voice, not loudness, are the qualities that will influen
your dog most.

Be consistent in the use of words during training. Confine your commands) as few words as possible and never change them. It is best for only one erson to carry on the dog's training, because different people will use ifferent words and tactics that will confuse your dog. The dog who hears come," "get over here," "hurry up," "here, Rex," and other commands hen he is wanted will become totally confused.

RAINING LESSONS

Training is hard on the dog — and on the trainer. A young dog just nnot take more than ten minutes of training at a stretch, so limit the ngth of your first lessons. Then you can gradually increase the length of me to about thirty minutes. You'll find that you too will tend to become npatient when you stretch out a training lesson. If you find yourself losing)ur temper, stop and resume the lesson at another time. Before and after ch lesson have a play period, but don't play during a training session. ven the youngest dog soon learns that schooling is a serious matter; fun)mes afterward.

Don't spend too much time on one phase of the training, or the dog will come bored. Always try to end a lesson on a pleasant note. Actually, in ne cases out of ten, if your dog isn't doing what you want it's because)u're not getting the idea over to him properly.

OUR TRAINING EQUIPMENT AND ITS USE

The leash is more properly called the lead, so we'll use that term here. he best leads for training are the six-foot webbed-cloth leads, usually ive-drab in color, and the six-foot leather lead. Fancier leads are available d may be used if desired.

You'll need a metal-link collar, called a choke chain, consisting of a metal ain with rings on each end. Even though the name may sound frightening, won't hurt your dog, and it is an absolute MUST in training. There is a ght and a wrong way to put the training collar on. It should go around the)g's neck so that you can attach the lead to the ring at the end of the ain which passes OVER, not under his neck. It is most important that e collar is put on properly so it will tighten when the lead is pulled and se when you relax your grip.

The correct way to hold the lead is also very important, as the collar ould have some slack in it, at all times, except when correcting. Holding e loop in your right hand, extend your arm out to the side, even with your oulder. With your left hand, grasp the lead as close as possible to the llar, without making it tight. The remaining portion of the lead can be ade into a loop which is held in the right hand. Keep this arm close to ur body. Most corrections will be made with the left hand by giving the ad a jerk in the direction you want the dog to go. The dog that pulls and rges ahead can be corrected by a steady pull on the lead.

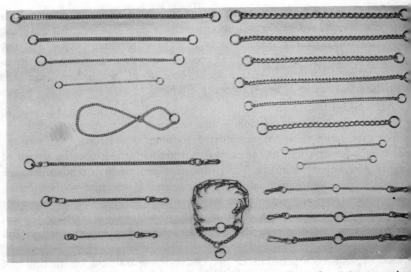

Special training collars for your dog can be purchased at your petsho

HEELING

"*Heeling*" in dog language means having your dog walk alongside you o
your left side, close to your leg, on lead or off. With patience and effort y
can train your dog to walk with you even on a crowded street or in th
presence of other dogs.

Now that you have learned the correct way to put on your dog's coll
and how to hold the lead, you are ready to start with his first lesson
heeling. Put the dog at your left side, sitting. Using the dog's name and t
command "*Heel*," start forward on your LEFT foot, giving a tug on t
lead to get the dog started. Always use the dog's name first, followed by t
command, such as "*Rex, heel*." Saying his name will help get his attenti
and will let him know that you are about to give a command.

Walk briskly, with even steps, going around in a large circle, square,
straight line. While walking, make sure that your dog stays on the l
side and close to your leg. If he lags behind, give several tugs on the le
to get him up to you, then praise him for doing well. If he forges ahead
swings wide, stop and jerk the lead sharply and bring him back to the prop
position. Always repeat the command when correcting, and praise him wh
he does well. If your dog continues to pull or lag behind, either yo
corrections are not severe enough or your timing between correction a
praise is off. Do this exercise for only five minutes at first, gradua
lengthening it to fifteen, or even half an hour.

To keep your dog's attention, talk to him as you keep him in place. You can also do a series of fast about-turns, giving the lead a jerk as you turn. He will gradually learn that he must pay attention or be jerked to your side. You can vary the routine by changing speeds, doing turns, figure-eights, and by zig-zagging across the training area.

"HEEL" MEANS "SIT," TOO

To the dog, the command "*Heel*" will also mean that he has to sit in the heel position at your left side when you stop walking — with no additional command from you. As you practice heeling, make him sit whenever you stop, at first using the word "*Sit*," then with no command at all. He'll soon get the idea and sit down when you stop and wait for the command "*Heel*" to start walking again.

TRAINING TO SIT

Training your dog to sit should be fairly easy. Stand him on your left side, holding the lead fairly short, and command him to "*Sit*." As you give the verbal command, pull up slightly with the lead and push his hindquarters down. Do not let him lie down or stand up. Keep him in a sitting position for a moment, then release the pressure on the lead and praise him. Constantly repeat the command as you hold him in a sitting position, thus fitting the word to the action in his mind. After a while he will begin to get the idea and will sit without your having to push his hindquarters down. When he reaches that stage, insist that he sit on command. If he is slow to obey, slap his hindquarters with your hand to get him down fast. *DO NOT HIT HIM HARD!* Teach him to sit on command facing you as well as when he is at your side. When he begins sitting on command with the lead on, try it with the lead off.

THE "LIE DOWN"

The object of this is to get the dog to lie down either on the verbal command "*Down*" or when you give him the hand signal, your hand raised in front of you, palm down. This is one of the most important parts of training. A well-trained dog will drop on command and stay down whatever the temptation: cat-chasing, car-chasing, or another dog across the street.

Don't start training to lie down until the dog is almost letter-perfect in sitting on command. Then place the dog in a sit, and kneel before him. With both hands, reach forward to his legs and take one front leg in each hand, thumbs up, and holding just below his elbows. Lift his legs slightly off the ground and pull them somewhat out in front of him. Simultaneously, give the command "*Down*" and lower his front legs to the ground.

Hold the dog down and stroke him to let him know that staying down is what you want him to do. This method is far better than forcing a young dog down. Using force can cause him to become very frightened and he will begin to dislike any training. Always talk to your dog and let him know that you are very pleased with him, and soon you will find that you have a happy working dog.

After he begins to get the idea, slide the lead under your left foot and give the command "*Down.*" At the same time, pull the lead. This will help get the dog down. Meanwhile, raise your hand in the down signal. Don't expect to accomplish all this in one session. Be patient and work with the dog. He'll cooperate if you show him just what you expect him to do.

THE "STAY"

The next step is to train your dog to stay either in a "*Sit*" or "*Down*" position. Sit him at your side. Give the command "*Stay,*" but be careful not to use his name with this command, because hearing his name may lead him to think that some action is expected of him. If he begins to move, repeat "*Stay*" firmly and hold him down in the sit. Constantly repeat the word "*Stay*" to fix the meaning of that command in his mind. After he has learned to stay for a short time, gradually increase the length of his stay. The hand signal for the stay is a downward sweep of your hand toward the dog's nose, with the palm facing him. While he is sitting, walk around him and stand in front of him. Hold the lead at first; later, drop the lead on the ground in front of him and keep him sitting. If he bolts, scold him and place him back in the same position, repeating the command and all the exercise.

Use some word such as "*Okay*" or "*Up*" to let him know when he can get up, and praise him well for a good performance. As this practice continues, walk farther and farther away from him. Later, try sitting him, giving the command to stay, and then walk out of sight, first for a few seconds, then for longer periods. A well-trained dog should stay where you put him without moving until you come and release him.

Similarly, practice having him stay in the down position, first with you near him, later when you step out of sight.

THE "COME" ON COMMAND

You can train your dog to come when you call him, if you begin when he is young. At first, work with him on lead. Sit the dog, then back away the length of the lead and call him, putting into your voice as much coaxing affection as possible. Give an easy tug on the lead to get him started. When he does come, make a big fuss over him; it might help at this point to give him a small piece of dog candy or food as a reward. He should get the idea soon. You can also move away from him the full length of the lead and call to him something like "*Rex, come,*" then run backward a few steps and stop, making him sit directly in front of you.

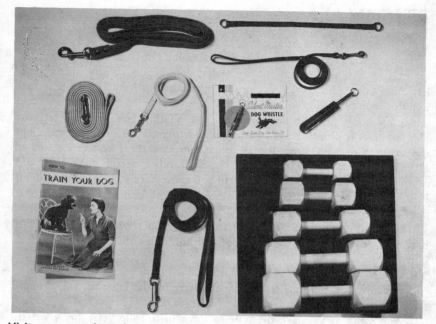

Visit your petshop for all of the training equipment you will need to make your pet a better canine citizen.

Don't be too eager to practice coming on command off lead. Wait until you are certain that you have the dog under perfect control before you try calling him when he's free. Once he gets the idea that he can disobey a command and get away with it, your training program will suffer a serious setback. Keep in mind that your dog's life may depend on his immediate response to a command to come when he is called. If he disobeys off lead, put the lead back on and correct him severely with jerks of the lead.

TEACHING TO COME TO HEEL

The object of this is for you to stand still, say "*Heel,*" and have your dog come right over to you and sit by your left knee in the heel position. If your dog has been trained to sit without command every time you stop, he's ready for this step.

Sit him in front of and facing you and step back one step. Moving only your left foot, pull the dog behind you, then step forward and pull him around until he is in a heel position. You can also have the dog go around by passing the lead behind your back. Use your left heel to straighten him out if he begins to sit behind you or crookedly. This may take a little work, but he will get the idea if you show him just what you want.

THE "STAND"

Your dog should be trained to stand in one spot without moving his feet, and he should allow a stranger to run his hand over his body and legs without showing any resentment or fear. Employ the same method you used in training him to stay on the sit and down. While walking, place your left hand out, palm toward his nose, and command him to stay. His first impulse will be to sit, so be prepared to stop him by placing your hand under his body, near his hindquarters, and holding him until he gets the idea that this is different from the command to sit. Praise him for standing, then walk to the end of the lead. Correct him strongly if he starts to move. Have a stranger approach him and run his hands over the dog's back and down his legs. Keep him standing until you come back to him. Walk around him from his left side, come to the heel position, and make sure that he does not sit until you command him to.

This is a very valuable exercise. If you plan to show your dog he will have learned to stand in a show pose and will allow the judge to examine him.

TRAINING SCHOOLS AND CLASSES

There are dog-training classes in all parts of the country, some sponsored by the local humane society.

If you feel that you lack the time or the skill to train your dog yourself, there are professional dog trainers who will do it for you, but basically dog training is a matter of training YOU and your dog to work together as a team, and if you don't do it yourself you will miss a lot of fun. Don't give up after trying unsuccessfully for a short time. Try a little harder and you and your dog will be able to work things out.

ADVANCED TRAINING AND OBEDIENCE TRIALS

Once you begin training your dog and you see how well he does, you'll probably be bitten by the "obedience bug" — the desire to enter him in obedience trials held under American Kennel Club auspices.

The A.K.C. obedience trials are divided into three classes: Novice, Open, and Utility.

In the Novice Class, the dog will be judged on the following basis:

TEST	MAXIMUM SCORE
Heel on lead	35
Stand for examination	30
Heel free — off lead	45
Recall (come on command)	30
One-minute sit (handler in ring)	30
Three-minute down (handler in ring)	30
Maximum total score	200

If the dog "qualifies" in three shows by earning at least 50% of the points for each test, with a total of at least 170 for the trial, he has earned the Companion Dog degree and the letters C.D. (Companion Dog) are entered after his name in the A.K.C. records.

After the dog has qualified as a C.D., he is eligible to enter the Open Class competition, where he will be judged on this basis:

TEST	MAXIMUM SCORE
Heel free	40
Drop on Recall	30
Retrieve (wooden dumbbell) on flat	25
Retrieve over obstacle (hurdle)	35
Broad jump	20
Three-minute sit (handler out of ring)	25
Five-minute down (handler out of ring)	25
Maximum total score	200

Again he must qualify in three shows for the C.D.X. (Companion Dog Excellent) title and then is eligible for the Utility Class, where he can earn the Utility Dog (U.D.) degree in these rugged tests:

TEST	MAXIMUM SCORE
Scent discrimination (picking up article handled by master from group) Article 1	20
Scent discrimination Article 2	20
Scent discrimination Article 3	20
Seek back (picking up an article dropped by handler)	30
Signal exercise (heeling, etc., on hand signal)	35
Directed jumping (over hurdle and bar jump)	40
Group examination	35
Maximum total score	200

For more complete information about these obedience trials, write for the American Kennel Club's *Regulations and Standards for Obedience Trials*. Dogs that are disqualified from breed shows because of alteration or physical defects are eligible to compete in these trials. Besides the formal A.K.C. obedience trials, there are informal "match" shows in which dogs compete for ribbons and inexpensive trophies. These shows are run by many local fanciers' dog clubs and by all-breed obedience clubs. In many localities the humane society and other groups conduct their own obedience shows. Your local petshop or kennel can keep you informed about such shows in your vicinity, and you will find them listed in the different dog magazines or in the pet column of your local newspaper.

6. Breeding

THE QUESTION OF SPAYING

If you feel that you will never want to raise a litter of purebred puppies, and if you do not wish to risk the possibility of an undesirable mating and surplus mongrel puppies inevitably destined for execution at the local pound, you may want to have your female spayed. Spaying is generally best performed after the female has passed her first heat and before her first birthday: this allows the female to attain the normal female characteristics, while still being young enough to avoid the possible complications encountered when an older female is spayed. A spayed female will remain a healthy, lively pet. You often hear that an altered female will become very fat. However, if you cut down on her food intake, she will not gain weight.

On the other hand, if you wish to show your dog (altered females are disqualified) or enjoy the excitement and feeling of accomplishment of breeding and raising a litter of puppies, particularly in your breed and from your pet, then definitely do not spay.

Male dogs, unlike tomcats, are almost never altered (castrated).

SEXUAL PHYSIOLOGY

Females usually reach sexual maturity (indicated by the first heat cycle, or season) at eight or nine months of age, but sexual maturity may occur as early as six months or as late as thirteen months of age. The average heat cycle (estrus period) lasts for twenty or twenty-one days, and occurs approximately every six months. For about five days immediately preceding the heat period, the female generally displays restlessness and an increased appetite. The vulva, or external genitals, begin to swell. The discharge, which is bright red at the onset and gradually becomes pale pink to straw in color, increases in quantity for several days and then slowly subsides, finally ceasing altogether. The vaginal discharge is subject to much variation: in some bitches it is quite heavy, in others it may never appear, and in some it may be so slight as to go unnoticed.

About eight or nine days after the first appearance of the discharge, the female becomes very playful with other dogs, but will not allow a mating to take place. Anywhere from the tenth or eleventh day, when the discharge has virtually ended and the vulva has softened, to the seventeenth or eighteenth day, the female will accept males and be able to conceive. Many biologists apply the term "heat" only to this receptive phase rather than to the whole estrus, as is commonly done by dog fanciers.

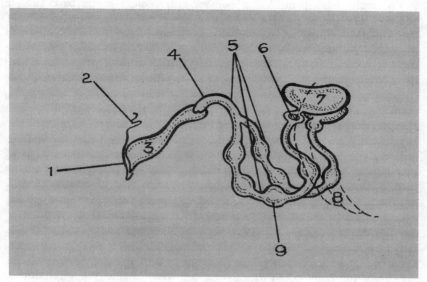

The reproduction system of the bitch: 1, vulva; 2, anus; 3, vagina; 4, cervix; 5, uterus; 6, ovary; 7, kidneys; 8, ribs; 9, fetal lump.

The ova (egg cells) from the female's ovaries are discharged into the oviduct toward the close of the acceptance phase, usually from the sixteenth to eighteenth day. From the eighteenth day until the end of the cycle, the female is still attractive to males, but she will repulse their advances. The entire estrus, however, may be quite variable: in some females vaginal bleeding ends and mating begins on the fourth day; in others, the discharge may continue throughout the entire cycle and the female will not accept males until the seventeenth day or even later.

The male dog — simply referred to by fanciers as the "dog," in contrast to the female, which is referred to as the "bitch" — upon reaching sexual maturity, usually at about six to eight months, is able, like other domesticated mammals, to breed at any time throughout the year.

The testes, the sperm-producing organs of the male, descend from the body cavity into the scrotum at birth. The condition of *cryptorchidism* refers to the retention of one or both testes within the body cavity. A testicle retained within the body cavity is in an environment too hot for it to function normally. A retained testicle may also become cancerous. If only one testicle descends, the dog is known as a *monorchid;* if neither descends, the dog is known as an *anorchid* (dog fanciers, however, refer to a dog with the latter condition as a cryptorchid). A monorchid dog is a fertile animal; an anorchid is sterile.

The male dog's penis has a bulbous enlargement at its base and, in addition, like the penis of a number of other mammals, contains a bone. When mating occurs, pressure on the penis causes a reflex action that fills the bulb with blood, swelling it to about five times its normal size within the female. This locks, or ties, the two animals together. After ejaculation, the animals usually remain tied for fifteen to thirty minutes, but they may separate very quickly or remain together an hour or more, depending on the length of time it takes for the blood to drain from the bulb.

CARE OF THE FEMALE IN ESTRUS

If you have a dog-proof run within your yard, it will be safe to leave your female in season there; if you don't have such a run, she should be shut indoors. Don't leave her alone outside even for a minute; she should be exercised only on lead. If you want to prevent the neighborhood dogs from congregating around your doorstep, as they inevitably will as soon as they discover that your female is in season, take her some distance from the house before you let her relieve herself. Take her in your car to a park or field for a chance to "stretch" her legs (always on lead of course). Keep watch for male dogs, and if one approaches take the female back to the car. After the three weeks are up you can let her out as before with no worry that she can have puppies until her next season.

Some owners find it simpler to board their female at a kennel until her season is over. However, it really is not difficult to watch your female at home. There are various products on the market which are useful at this time. Although the female in season keeps herself quite clean, sometimes she unavoidably stains furniture or rugs. You can buy sanitary belts made especially for dogs at your petshop. Consult your veterinarian for information on pills to be taken to check odor during this period. There also is a pill that prevents the female from coming in season for extended periods, and there are many different types of liquids, powders, and sprays of varying efficiency used to keep male dogs away. However, the one safe rule (whatever products you use) is: keep your bitch away from dogs that could mount her.

SHOULD YOU BREED YOUR MALE?

As with every question, whether or not to use a male dog as a stud has two sides. The arguments for and against using a dog as a stud are often very close to the ridiculous. A classic example would be the tale that once you use a dog as a stud he will lose his value as a show dog or any one of the other functions a dog may have. A sound rule may well be: *if you have a stud who has proven his worth at the shows, place his services out for hire, if only for the betterment of the breed; if your dog is not of show quality, do not use him as a stud.*

Top champion studs can bring their owners many dollars in breeding revenue. If the stud is as good as you feel he is, his services will soon be

great demand. Using a dog as a stud will not lower his value in other
nctions in any way. Many breeders will permit a male dog to breed an
:perienced female once, when about a year old, and then they begin to
ow their stud until he has gained his conformation championship. He is
en placed out for hire through advertising in the various bulletins, journals,
d show catalogs, and through the stud registers maintained by many pet-
ops.

HOULD YOU BREED YOUR FEMALE?

If you are an amateur and decide to breed your female it would be wise
• talk with a breeder and find out all that breeding and caring for puppies
tails. You must be prepared to assume the responsibility of caring for
e mother through her pregnancy and for the puppies until they are of
leable age. Raising a litter of puppies can be a rewarding experience, but
means work as well as fun, and there is no guarantee of financial profit.
s the puppies grow older and require more room and care, the amateur
eeder, in desperation, often sells the puppies for much less than they
re worth; sometimes he has to give them away. If the cost of keeping the
uppies will drain your finances, think twice.

If you have given careful consideration to all these things and still want
breed your female, remember that there is some preparation necessary
efore taking this step.

WHEN TO BREED

It is usually best to breed in the second or third season. Consider when
he puppies will be born and whether their birth and later care will inter-
ere with your work or vacation plans. Gestation period is approximately
ifty-eight to sixty-three days. Allow enough time to select the right stud
or her. Don't be in a position of having to settle for any available male
f she comes into season sooner than expected. Your female will probably
e ready to breed twelve days after the first colored discharge. You can
usually make arrangements to board her with the owner of the male for
a few days to insure her being there at the proper time, or you can take
her to be mated and bring her home the same day. If she still appears
receptive she may be bred again a day or two later. Some females never
show signs of willingness, so it helps to have the experience of a breeder.
The second day after the discharge changes color is the proper time; she
may be bred for about three days following. For an additional week or so
she may have some discharge and attract other dogs by her odor, but she
can seldom be bred at this time.

HOW TO SELECT A STUD

Choose a mate for your female with an eye to countering her deficiencies.
If possible, both male and female should have several ancestors in common

within the last two or three generations, as such combinations generall "click" best. The male should have a good show record himself or be the sire of champions. The owner of the stud usually charges a fee for the us of the dog. The fee varies. Payment of a fee does not guarantee a litter but it does generally confer the right to breed your female again to the stud if she does not have puppies the first time. In some cases the owne of the stud will agree to take a choice puppy in place of a stud fee. Yo and the owner of the stud should settle all details beforehand, including such questions as what age the puppies should reach before the stud' owner can make his choice, what disposition is made of a single surviving puppy under an agreement by which the stud owner has pick of the litter and so on. In all cases it is best that the agreement entered into by bitcl owner and stud owner be in the form of a written contract.

It is customary for the female to be sent to the male; if the stud dog of your choice lives any distance you will have to make arrangements to have your female shipped to him. The quickest way is by air, and if you call your nearest airport the airline people will give you information as to the best and fastest flight. Some airlines furnish their own crates for shipping, whereas others require that you furnish your own. The owner of the stud will make the arrangements for shipping the female back to you. You have to pay all shipping charges.

PREPARATION FOR BREEDING

Before you breed your female, make sure she is in good health. She should be neither too thin nor too fat. Skin diseases must be cured before breeding; a bitch with skin diseases can pass them on to her puppies. If she has worms she should be wormed before being bred, or within three weeks afterward. It is a good idea to have your veterinarian give her a booster shot for distemper and hepatitis before the puppies are born. This will increase the immunity the puppies receive during their early, most vulnerable period. Choose a dependable veterinarian and rely on him if there is an emergency when your female whelps.

HOW OFTEN SHOULD YOU BREED YOUR FEMALE?

Do not breed your bitch after she reaches six years of age. If you wish to breed her several times while she is young, it is wise to breed her only once a year. In other words, breed her, skip a season, and then breed her again. This will allow her to gain back her full strength between whelpings.

THE IMPORTANCE AND APPLICATION OF GENETICS

Any person attempting to breed dogs should have a basic understanding of the transmission of traits, or characteristics, from the parents to the offspring and some familiarity with the more widely used genetic terms that he will probably encounter. A knowledge of the fundamental mechanics of enetics enables a breeder to better comprehend the passing, complementing, nd covering of both good points and faults from generation to generation. t enables him to make a more judicial and scientific decision in selecting otential mates.

Inheritance, fundamentally, is due to the existence of microscopic units, nown as *GENES,* present in the cells of all individuals. Genes somehow ontrol the biochemical reactions that occur within the embryo or adult rganism. This control results in changing or guiding the development of he organism's characteristics. A "string" of attached genes is known as a *CHROMOSOME.* With a few important exceptions, every chromosome has a partner chromosome carrying a duplicate or equivalent set of genes. Each gene, therefore, has a partner gene, known as an *ALLELE.* The number of different pairs of chromosomes present in the cells of the organism varies with the type of organism: a certain parasitic worm has only one pair, a certain fruit fly has four different pairs, man has 23 different pairs, and your dog has 39 different pairs per cell. Because each chromosome may have many hundreds of genes, a single cell of the body may contain a total of several thousand genes. Heredity is obviously a very complex matter.

In the simplest form of genetic inheritance, one particular gene and its duplicate, or allele, on the partner chromosome control a single characteristic. The presence of freckles in the human skin, for example, is believed to be due to the influence of a single pair of genes.

Each cell of the body contains the specific number of paired chromosomes characteristic of the organism. Because each type of gene is present on both chromosomes of a chromosome pair, *each type of gene is therefore present in duplicate.* The fusion of a sperm cell from the male with an egg cell from the female, as occurs in fertilization, should therefore result in offspring having a *quadruplicate number* (4) of each type of gene. Mating of these individuals would then produce progeny having an *octuplicate number* (8) of each type of gene, and so on. This, however, is normally prevented by a special process. When ordinary body cells prepare to divide to form more tissue, each pair of chromosomes duplicates itself so that there are four partner chromosomes of each kind instead of only two. When the cell divides, two of the four partners, or one pair, go into each new cell. This process, known as *MITOSIS,* insures that each new body cell contains the proper number of chromosomes. Reproductive cells (sperm cell and egg cells), however, undergo a special kind of division known as *MEIOSIS.* In meiosis, the chromosome pairs do *not* duplicate themselves, and thus when the reproductive cells reach the final dividing stage only one chromosome, or one-half of the pair, goes into each new reproductive cell. Each reproductive cell, therefore, has only half the normal number of chromosomes. These are referred to as *HAPLOID* cells, in contrast to *DIPLOID* cells, which have the full number of chromosomes.

47

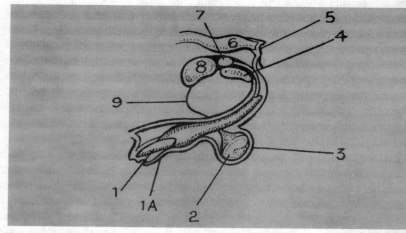

The reproductive system of a male: 1a, sheath; 1, penis; 2, testicle; scrotum; 4, pelvic bone; 5, anus; 6, rectum; 7, prostate; 8, bladder; vas deferens.

When the haploid sperm cell fuses with the haploid egg cell in fertilization, the resulting offspring has the normal diploid number of chromosomes.

If both partner genes, or alleles, affect the trait in an identical manner, the genes are said to be *HOMOZYGOUS*, but if one affects the character in a manner different from the other gene, or allele, the genes are said to be *HETEROZYGOUS*. For example, in the pair of genes affecting eye color in humans, if each gene of the pair produces blue eyes, the genes (and also the person carrying the genes) are said to be homozygous for blue eyes. If, however, one gene of the pair produces blue eyes, while the other gene, or allele, produces brown eyes, they are said to be heterozygous. The presence of heterozygous genes raises the question, *"Will the offspring have blue eyes or brown eyes?"* which in turn introduces another genetic principle: *DOMINANCE* and *RECESSIVENESS*.

If one gene of a pair can block the action of its partner, or allele, while still producing its own affect, that gene is said to be *dominant* over its allele. Its allele, on the other hand, is said to be recessive. In the case of heterozygous genes for eye color, the brown eye gene is dominant over the recessive blue eye gene, and the offspring therefore will have brown eyes. Much less common is the occurrence of gene pairs in which neither gene is completely dominant over the other. This, known as *INCOMPLETE* or *PARTIAL DOMINANCE*, results in a blending of the opposing influences. In cattle, if a homozygous (pure) red bull is mated with a homozygous (pure) white cow, the calf will be roan, a blending of red and white hairs in its coat, rather than either all red or all white.

During meiosis, or division of the reproductive (sperm and egg) cells, each pair of chromosomes splits, and one-half of each pair goes into one of the two new cells. Thus, in the case of eye color genes, one new reproductive cell will get the chromosome carrying the blue eye gene, while the other new reproductive cell will get the chromosome carrying the brown eye gene, and so on for each pair of chromosomes. If an organism has only two pairs of chromosomes — called pair A, made up of chromosomes A_1 and A_2, and pair B, made up of chromosomes B_1 and B_2 — each new reproductive cell will get one chromosome from each pair, and four different combinations are possible: A_1 and B_1; A_1 and B_2; A_2 and B_1, or A_2 and B_2. If the blue eye gene is on A_1, the brown eye gene on A_2, the gene for curly hair on B_1 and the gene for straight hair on B_2, each of the above combinations will exert a different genetic effect on the offspring. This different grouping of chromosomes in the new reproductive cell as a result of meiotic cell division is known as *INDEPENDENT ASSORTMENT* and is one reason why variation occurs in the offspring. In the dog, with 39 pairs of chromosomes, the possibilities of variation through independent assortment are tremendous.

But variation does not end here. For example, if two dominant genes, such as the genes for brown eyes and dark hair, were on the same chromosome, all brown-eyed people would have dark hair. Yet in instances where such joined or *LINKED* genes do occur, the two characteristics do not always appear together in the same offspring. This is due to a process known as *CROSS-OVER* or *RECOMBINATION*. Recombination is the mutual exchange of corresponding blocks of genes between the two chromosomes in a pair. That is, during cell division, the two chromosomes may exchange their tip sections or other corresponding segments. If the segments exchanged contain the eye color genes, the brown eye gene will be transferred from the chromosome carrying the dark hair gene to the chromosome carrying the light hair gene, and then brown eyes will occur with light hair, provided that the individual is homozygous for the recessive light hair gene.

Another important source of variation is *MUTATION*. In mutation, a gene becomes altered, such as by exposure to irradiation, and exerts a different effect than it did before. Most mutations are harmful to the organism, and some may result in death. Offspring carrying mutated genes and showing the effects of these mutations are known as *MUTANTS* or *SPORTS*. Mutation also means that instead of only two alleles for eye color, such as brown and blue, there may now be three or more (gray, black, etc.) creating a much larger source for possible variation in the offspring.

Further complications in the transmission and appearance of genetic traits are the phenomena known as *EPISTASIS* and *PLEIOTROPY*. Epistasis refers to a gene exerting influence on genes other than its own allele.

In all-white red-eyed (albino) guinea pigs, for example, the gene controlling intensity of color is epistatic to any other color gene and prevents that gene from producing its effect. Thus, even if a gene for red spots were present in the cells of the guinea pig, the color intensity gene would prevent the red spots from appearing in the guinea pig's white coat. *Pleiotropy* refers to the fact that a single gene may control a number of characteristics. In the fruit fly, for example, the gene that controls eye color may also affect the structure of certain body parts and even the lifespan of the insect.

One special pair of chromosomes is known as the sex chromosomes. In man, dog, and other mammals, these chromosomes are of two types, designated as X and Y. Under normal conditions, a mammal carrying two X-type sex chromosomes is a female, whereas a mammal carrying one X-type and one Y-type is a male. Females, therefore, have only X chromosomes and can only contribute X chromosomes to the offspring, but the male may contribute either an X or a Y.

If the male's sperm carrying an X chromosome fertilizes the female's egg cell (X), the offspring (XX) will be female; if a sperm carrying a Y chromosome fertilizes the egg (X), the offspring (XY) will be male. It is the male, therefore, that determines the sex of the offspring in mammals.

Traits controlled by genes present on the sex chromosome, and which appear in only one sex, are said to be *SEX LINKED*. If, for example, a rare recessive gene occurs on the X chromosome, it cannot exert its effect in the female because the dominant allele on the other X chromosome will counteract it. In the male, however, there is no second X chromosome, and if the Y chromosome cannot offer any countereffect, the recessive character will appear. There are also *SEX-LIMITED* characteristics: these appear primarily or solely in one sex, but the genes for these traits are not carried on the sex chromosomes. Sex-limited traits appear when genes on other chromosomes exert their effect in the proper hormonal (male or female) environment. Sex-linked and sex-limited transmission is how a trait may skip a generation, by being passed from grandfather to grandson through a mother in which the trait, though present, does not show.

In dealing with the simplest form of heredity — one gene effecting one character — there is an expected ratio of the offspring displaying the character to those who do not display it, depending upon the genetic makeup of the parents. If a parent is homozygous for a character, such as blue eyes, it makes no difference which half of the chromosome pair enters the new reproductive cell, because each chromosome carries the gene for blue eyes. If a parent is heterozygous, however, one reproductive cell will receive the brown eye gene while the other will receive the blue eye gene. If both parents are homozygous for blue eyes, all the offspring will receive two blue eye genes, and all will have blue eyes. If a parent is homozygous for blue eyes, and the other parent is homozygous for brown eyes, all the offspring will be heterozygous, receiving one brown eye gene and one blue eye gene, and because brown is dominant, all will have brown eyes. If both parents are heterozygous, both the blue eye gene and the brown eye gene from one parent have an equal likelihood of ending up with either the blue eye or the brown eye gene from the other parent. This results in a ratio of two heterozygous offspring to the one homozygous for brown eyes and one homozygous for blue eyes, giving a total genetic, or genotypic, ratio of $2:1:1$ or, as it is more commonly arranged, $1:2:1$. As the two heterozygous as well as the homozygous brown eye offspring will have brown eyes, the ratio of brown eyes to blue eyes (or phenotypic ratio) will be $3:1$.

If one parent is heterozygous and the other parent is homozygous for the recessive gene for blue eyes, half of the offspring will be homozygous for blue eyes and will have blue eyes, but the other half of the offspring will be heterozygous and have brown eyes. (Here both the genotypic and phenotypic ratio is $1:1$.)

If the homozygous parent, however, has the dominant gene (brown eyes), half of the offspring will be heterozygous and half will be homozygous, as before, but all will have brown eyes. By repeated determinations of these ratios in the offspring, geneticists are able to analyze the genetic makeup of the parents.

Before leaving heredity, it might be well to explain the difference between inbreeding, outcrossing, line breeding, and similar terms. Basically, there are only inbreeding and outbreeding. Inbreeding, however, according to its intensity, is usually divided into inbreeding proper and line breeding. Inbreeding proper is considered to be the mating of very closely related individuals, generally within the immediate family, but this is sometimes extended to include matings to first cousins and grandparents. Line breeding is the mating of more distantly related animals, that is, animals, not immediately related to each other but having a common ancestor, such as the same grandsire or great-grandsire. Outbreeding is divided into outcrossing, which is the mating of dogs from different families within the same breed, and cross-breeding, which is mating purebred dogs from different breeds.

From the foregoing discussion of genetics, it should be realized that the theory of telegony, which states that the sire of one litter can influence future litters sired by other studs, is simply not true; it is possible, however, if several males mate with a female during a single estrus cycle, that the various puppies in the litter may have different sires (but not two sires for any one puppy). It should also be realized that blood does not really enter into the transmission of inheritance, although people commonly speak of "bloodlines," "pure-blooded," etc.

7. Care of the Mother and Family

PRENATAL CARE OF THE FEMALE

You can expect the puppies nine weeks from the day of breeding, although 58 days is as common as 63. During this time the female should receive normal care and exercise. If she is overweight, don't increase her food at first; excess weight at whelping time is not good. If she is on the thin side, build her up, giving her a morning meal of cereal and egg yolk. Consult your veterinarian as to increasing her vitamins and mineral supplement. During the last weeks the puppies grow enormously, and the mother will have little room for food and less appetite. Divide her meals into smaller portions and feed her more ofen. If she loses her appetite, tempt her with meat, liver, chicken, etc.

As she grows heavier, eliminate violent exercise and jumping. Do not eliminate exercise entirely, as walking is beneficial to the female in whelp, and mild exercise will maintain her muscle tone in preparation for the birth. Weigh your female after breeding and keep a record of her weight each week thereafter. Groom your bitch daily — some females have a slight discharge during gestation, more prevalent during the last two weeks, so wash the vulva with warm water daily. Usually, by the end of the fifth week you can notice a broadening across her loins, and her breasts become firmer. By the end of the sixth week your veterinarian can tell you whether or not she is pregnant.

PREPARATION OF WHELPING QUARTERS

Prepare a whelping box at least a week before the puppies are to arrive and allow the mother-to-be to sleep there overnight or to spend some time in it during the day to become accustomed to it. She is then less likely to try to have her litter under the front porch or in the middle of your bed.

The box should have a wooden floor. Sides should be high enough to keep the puppies in but low enough to allow the mother to get out after she has fed them. Layers of newspapers spread over the whole area will make excellent bedding and will be absorbent enough to keep the surface warm and dry. They should be removed when wet or soiled and replaced with another thick layer. An old quilt or blanket is more comfortable for the mother and makes better footing for the nursing puppies, at least during the first week, than slippery newspaper. The quilt should be secured firmly.

SUPPLIES TO HAVE ON HAND

As soon as you have the whelping box prepared, set up the nursery by collecting the various supplies you will need when the puppies arrive. You

uld have the following items on hand: a box lined with towels for the
ppies, a heating pad or hot water bottle to keep the puppy box warm,
ile of clean terrycloth towels or washcloths to remove membranes and
dry puppies, a stack of folded newspapers, a roll of paper towels, vase-
e, rubber gloves, soap, iodine, muzzle, cotton balls, a small pair of
unt scissors to cut umbilical cords (stick them into an open bottle of
ohol so they keep freshly sterilized), a rectal thermometer, white thread,
flashlight in case the electricity goes off, a waste container, and a scale
weighing each puppy at birth.

It is necessary that the whelping room be warm and free from drafts,
cause puppies are delivered wet from the mother. Keep a little notebook
d pencil handy so you can record the duration of the first labor and the
ne between the arrival of each puppy. If there is trouble in whelping,
is is the information that the veterinarian will want. Keep his telephone
mber handy in case you have to call him in an emergency, and warn him
be prepared for an emergency, should you need him.

HELPING

Be prepared for the actual whelping several days in advance. Usually the
male will tear up papers, try to dig nests, refuse food, and generally act
stless and nervous. These may be false alarms; the real test is her tem-
rature, which will drop to below 100° about twelve hours before whelp-
g. Take her temperature rectally at a set time each day, starting about
week before she is due to whelp. After her temperature goes down, keep
r constantly with you or put her in the whelping box and stay in the
om with her. She will seem anxious and look to you for reassurance.
e prepared to remove the membranes covering the puppy's head if the
other fails to do this, for the puppy could smother otherwise.

The mother should start licking the puppy as soon as it is out of the
c, thus drying and stimulating it, but if she does not perform this task
ou can do it with a soft rough towel, instead. The afterbirth should follow
ne birth of each puppy, attached to the puppy by the umbilical cord. Watch
) make sure that each is expelled, for retaining this material can cause
nfection. The mother probably will eat the afterbirth after biting the
ord. One or two will not hurt her; they stimulate milk supply as well as
abor for remaining puppies. Too many, however, can make her lose her
ppetite for the food she needs to feed her puppies and regain her strength,
o remove the rest of them along with the soiled newspapers, and keep the
ox dry and clean to relieve her anxiety.

If a puppy does not start breathing, wrap him in a towel, hold him upside
lown with his head toward the ground, and shake him vigorously. If he
till does not breathe, rub his ribs briskly; if this also fails, administer
rtificial respiration by compressing the ribs about twenty times per minute.

53

If the mother does not bite the cord, or bites it too close to the body you should take over the job to prevent an umbilical hernia. Cut the cord a short distance from the body with your blunt scissors. Put a drop iodine on the end of the cord; it will dry up and fall off in a few days

The puppies should follow each other at regular intervals, but deliveries can be as short as five minutes or as long as two hours apart. A puppy may be presented backwards; if the mother does not seem to be in trouble, do not interfere. But if enough of the puppy is outside the birth canal, use a rough towel and help her by pulling gently on the puppy. Pull only when she pushes. A rear-first, or breech, birth can cause a puppy to strangle on its own umbilical cord, so don't let the mother struggle too long. Breech birth is quite common.

When you think all the puppies have been whelped, have your veterinarian examine the mother to determine if all the afterbirths have been expelled. He will probably give her an injection to be certain that the uterus is clean, a shot of calcium for prevention of eclampsia, and possibly an injection of penicillin to prevent infection.

RAISING THE PUPPIES

Hold each puppy to a breast as soon as you have dried him. This will be an opportunity to have a good meal without competition. Then place him in the small box that you have prepared so he will be out of his mother's way while she is whelping. Keep a record of birth weights and take weekly readings thereafter so that you will have an accurate account of the puppies' growth. After the puppies have arrived, take the mother outside for a walk and a drink, and then leave her to take care of them. Offer her a dish of vanilla ice cream or milk with corn syrup in it. She usually will eat lying down while the puppies are nursing and will appreciate the coolness of the ice cream during warm weather or in a hot room. She will not want to stay away from her puppies more than a minute or two the first few weeks. Be sure to keep water available at all times, and feed her milk or broth frequently, as she needs liquids to produce milk. To encourage her to eat, offer her the foods she likes best, until she "asks" to be fed without your tempting her. She will soon develop a ravenous appetite and should be fed whenever she is hungry.

Be sure that all the puppies are getting enough to eat. Cut their claws with special dog "nail" clippers, as they grow rapidly and scratch the mother as the puppies nurse. Normally the puppies should be completely weaned by six weeks, although you may start to give them supplementary feedings at three weeks. They will find it easier to lap semi-solid food.

As the puppies grow up, the mother will go into the box only to nurse them, first sitting up and then standing. To dry up her milk supply completely, keep her away from her puppies for longer periods. After a few days of part-time nursing she will be able to stay away for much longer riods of time, and then completely. The little milk left will be resorbed.

When the puppies are five weeks old, consult your veterinarian about mporary shots to protect them against distemper and hepatitis; it is uite possible for dangerous infectious germs to reach them even though ou keep their living quarters sanitary. You can expect the puppies to need : least one worming before they are ready to go to their new homes, so ke a stool sample to your veterinarian before they are three weeks old. one puppy has worms, all should be wormed. Follow your veterinarian's dvice.

The puppies may be put outside, unless it is too cold, as soon as their yes are open (about ten days), and they will benefit from the sunlight. A ibber mat or newspapers underneath their box will protect them from old or dampness.

OW TO TAKE CARE OF A LARGE LITTER

The size of a litter varies greatly. If your bitch has a large litter she may ave trouble feeding all of the puppies. You can help her by preparing n extra puppy box. Leave half the litter with the mother and the other alf in a warm place, changing their places at two-hour intervals at first. ater you may change them less frequently, leaving them all together except luring the day. Try supplementary feeding, too, as soon as their eyes are pen.

AESAREAN SECTION

If your female goes into hard labor and is not able to give birth within wo hours, you will know that there is something wrong. Call your veterinarian for advice. Some females must have Caesarean sections (taking puppies from the mother by surgery), but don't be alarmed if your dog has o undergo this. The operation is relatively safe. She can be taken to the veterinarian, operated on, and then be back in her whelping box at home within three hours, with all puppies nursing normally a short time later.

8. Health

WATCHING YOUR PUPPY'S HEALTH

First, don't be frightened by the number of diseases a dog can contrac The majority of dogs never get any of them. Don't become a dog-hypocho driac. All dogs have days when they feel lazy and want to lie around doi nothing. For the few diseases that you might be concerned about, rememb that your veterinarian is your dog's best friend. When you first get yo puppy, select a veterinarian who you feel is qualified to treat dogs. I will get to know your dog and will be glad to have you consult him f advice. A dog needs little medical care, but that little is essential to h good health and well-being. He needs:

1. Proper diet at regular hours
2. Clean, roomy housing
3. Daily exercise
4. Companionship and love
5. Frequent grooming
6. Regular check-ups by your veterinarian

THE USEFUL THERMOMETER

Almost every serious ailment shows itself by an increase in the dog's bod temperature. If your dog acts lifeless, looks dull-eyed, and gives the impres sion of illness, check his temperature by using a rectal thermometer. Hol the dog and insert the thermometer, which should be lubricated with vase line, and take a reading. The average normal temperature is 101.5° F Excitement may raise this value slightly, but any rise of more than a fev points is a cause for alarm. Consult your veterinarian.

FIRST AID

In general, a dog will heal his wounds by licking them. If he swallow anything harmful, chances are that he will throw it up. But it will probabl make you feel better to help him if he is hurt, so treat his wounds as yo would your own. Wash out the dirt and apply an antiseptic. If you are afraid that your dog has swallowed poison and you can't get to the veteri narian fast enough, try to induce vomiting by giving him a strong solutior of salt water or mustard and water. Amateur diagnosis is dangerous because the symptoms of so many dog diseases are alike. Too many peopl wait too long to take their dog to the doctor.

IMPORTANCE OF INOCULATIONS

With the proper series of inoculations, your dog will be almost completely protected against disease. However, it occasionally happens that the sho

es not take, and sometimes a different form of the virus appears against
ich your dog may not be protected.

STEMPER

Probably the most virulent of all dog diseases is distemper. Young dogs
: most susceptible to it, although it may affect dogs of all ages. The dog
ll lose his appetite, seem depressed, chilled, and run a fever. Often he
ll have a watery discharge from his eyes and nose. Unless treated
omptly, the disease goes into advanced stages with infections of the lungs,
estines, and nervous system, and dogs that recover may be left with some
pairment such as paralysis, convulsions, a twitch, or some other defect,
ually spastic in nature. The best protection against this is very early
oculation with a series of permanent shots and a booster shot each year
ereafter.

EPATITIS

Veterinarians report an increase in the spread of this viral disease in
cent years, usually with younger dogs as the victims. The initial symptoms
- drowsiness, vomiting, great thirst, loss of appetite, and a high tempera-
re — closely resemble those of distemper. These symptoms are often
companied by swellings of the head, neck, and abdomen. The disease
rikes quickly; death may occur in just a few hours. Protection is afforded
y injection with a vaccine recently developed.

EPTOSPIROSIS

This disease is caused by bacteria that live in stagnant or slow-moving
ater. It is carried by rats and dogs; infection is begun by the dog's licking
bstances contaminated by the urine or feces of infected animals. The
mptoms are diarrhea and a yellowish-brown discoloration of the jaws,
ngue, and teeth, caused by an inflammation of the kidneys. This disease
an be cured if caught in time, but it is best to ward it off with a vaccine
hich your veterinarian can administer along with the distemper shots.

ABIES

This is an acute disease of the dog's central nervous system. It is spread
y infectious saliva transmitted by the bite of an infected animal. Rabies
generally manifested in one of two classes of symptoms. The first is
furious rabies," in which the dog shows a period of melancholy or depres-
on, then irritation, and finally paralysis. The first period lasts from a few
ours to several days. During this time the dog is cross and will change his
osition often. He loses his appetite for food and begins to lick, bite,
nd swallow foreign objects. During the irritative phase the dog is spas-
odically wild and has impulses to run away. He acts in a fearless manner
nd runs and bites at everything in sight. If he is caged or confined he will
ght at the bars, often breaking teeth or fracturing his jaw. His bark becomes
peculiar howl. In the final, or paralytic, stage, the animal's lower jaw

becomes paralyzed and hangs down; he walks with a stagger and sali
drips from his mouth. Within four to eight days after the onset of par
lysis, the dog dies.

The second class of symptoms is referred to as "dumb rabies" and
characterized by the dog's walking in a bearlike manner, head down. T
lower jaw is paralyzed and the dog is unable to bite. Outwardly it may see
as though he had a bone caught in his throat.

Even if your pet should be bitten by a rabid dog or other animal,
probably can be saved if you get him to the veterinarian in time for
series of injections. However, after the symptoms have appeared no cu
is possible. But remember that an annual rabies inoculation is almo
certain protection against rabies. If you suspect your dog of rabies, noti
your local Health Department. A rabid dog is a danger to all who con
near him.

COUGHS, COLDS, BRONCHITIS, PNEUMONIA

Respiratory diseases may affect the dog because he is forced to liv
under man-made conditions rather than in his natural environment. Bein
subjected to cold or a draft after a bath, sleeping near an air conditione
or in the path of a fan or near a radiator can cause respiratory ailment
The symptoms are similar to those in humans. The germs of these disease
however, are different and do not affect both dogs and humans, so the
cannot be infected by each other. Treatment is much the same as for
child with the same type of illness. Keep the dog warm, quiet, and we
fed. Your veterinarian has antibiotics and other remedies to help the do
recover.

INTERNAL PARASITES

There are four common internal parasites that may infect your dog
These are roundworms, hookworms, whipworms, and tapeworms. The firs
three can be diagnosed by laboratory examination; the presence of tapeworms is determined by seeing segments in the stool or attached to the hai
around the tail. Do not under any circumstances attempt to worm you
dog without the advice of your veterinarian. After first determining wha
type of worm or worms are present, he will advise you of the best method
of treatment.

EXTERNAL PARASITES

The dog that is groomed regularly and provided with clean sleeping
quarters should not be troubled by fleas, ticks, or lice. If the dog should
become infested with any of these parasites, he should be treated with a
medicated dip bath or the new oral medications that are presently available.

SKIN AILMENTS

Any persistent scratching may indicate an irritation. Whenever you groom
your dog, look for the reddish spots that may indicate eczema, mange, or
fungal infection. Rather than treating your dog yourself, take him to the

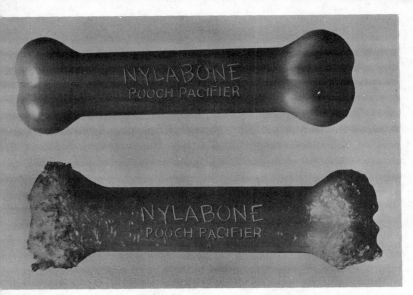

NYLABONE® is a necessity that is available at your local petshop (not in supermarkets). The puppy or grown dog chews the hambone flavored nylon into a frilly dog toothbrush, massaging his gums and cleaning his teeth as he plays. Veterinarians highly recommend this product . . . but beware of cheap imitations which might splinter or break.

veterinarian, as some of the conditions may be difficult to eradicate and can cause permanent damage to his coat.

EYES, EARS, TEETH, AND CLAWS

If you notice foreign matter collecting in the corners of your dog's eyes, wipe it out with a piece of cotton or tissue. If there is a discharge, check with your veterinarian.

Examine your dog's ears daily. Remove all visible wax, using a piece of cotton dipped in a boric acid solution or a solution of equal parts of water and hydrogen peroxide. Be gentle and don't probe into the ear, but just clean the parts you can see.

Don't give your dog bones to chew: they can choke him or puncture his intestines. Today veterinarians and dog experts recommend Nylabone, a synthetic bone manufactured by a secret process, that can't splinter or break even when pounded by a hammer. Nylabone will keep puppies from chewing furniture, aid in relieving the aching gums of a teething pup, and act as a toothbrush for the older dog, preventing the accumulation of tartar. Check your dog's mouth regularly and, as he gets older, have your veterinarian clean his teeth twice a year.

To clip your dog's claws, use specially designed clippers that are available at your petshop. Never take off too much of the claw, as you might

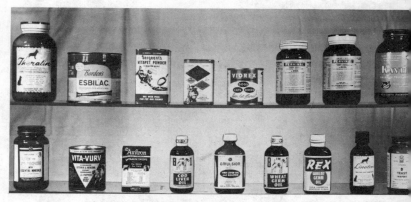

Active dogs and breeding bitches need food supplements. Visit yo
petshop for fresh vitamins and minerals to be added to your dog's di

cut the quick, which is sensitive and will bleed. Be particularly careful wh
you cut claws in which the quick is not visible. If you have any doub
about being able to cut your dog's claws, have your veterinarian or petsh
do it periodically.

CARE OF THE AGED DOG

With the increased knowledge and care available, there is no reason w
your dog should not live to a good old age. As the years go by he m
need a little additional care. Remember that an excessively fat dog is n
healthy, particularly as he grows older, so limit the older dog's food accor
ingly. He needs exercise as much as ever, although his heart cannot be
the strain of sudden and violent exertion. Failing eyesight or hearing mea
lessened awareness of dangers, so you must protect him more than eve

Should you decide at this time to get a puppy, to avoid being witho
a dog when your old friend is no longer with you, be very careful ho
you introduce the puppy. He naturally will be playful and will expect t
older dog to respond to his advances. Sometimes the old dog will get
new lease on life from a new puppy, but he may be consumed with jealous
Do not give the newcomer the attention that formerly was exclusively t
older dog's. Feed them apart, and show your old friend that you still lo
him the most; the puppy, not being accustomed to individual attention, wi
not mind sharing your love.

9. Showing

There is no greater pleasure for the owner than showing a beautiful dog perfectly groomed and trained for the show ring. Whether he wins or not, it is gratifying to show a dog in superb condition, one that is a credit to your training and care. A great deal of preparation, both for you and your dog, is needed before the day that you do any serious winning. Showing is not so easy as it looks, even if you have a magnificent dog. He must be presented to the judge so that all of his good points are shown to advantage. This requires practice in gaiting, daily grooming from puppyhood, and the proper diet to make him sound in body.

When you buy your puppy you probably will think he is the best in the country and possibly in the world, but before you enter the highly competitive world of dog shows, get some unbiased expert opinion. As your dog matures, compare him with the standard of his breed. Visit a few dog shows as a spectator and make mental notes of what is required of the handlers and dogs. Watch how the experienced handlers manage their dogs to bring out their best points.

TYPES OF DOG SHOWS

There are various types of dog shows. The American Kennel Club sanctioned matches are shows at which purebred dogs may compete, but not for championship points. These are excellent for you to enter to accustom you and your dog to showing. If your dog places in a few match shows, then you might seriously consider entering the big-time shows. An American Kennel Club all-breed show is one at which purebred dogs compete for championship points. An American Kennel Club specialty show is for one breed only. It may be held in conjunction with an all-breed show (by designating the classes at that show as its specialty show) or it may be held entirely apart. Obedience trials are different in that in them the dog is judged according to his obedience and ability to perform, not by his conformation to the breed standard.

There are two types of championship conformation shows: *benched* and *unbenched*. At a benched show your dog must be on his appointed bench during the advertised hours of the show's duration. He may be removed from the bench only to be taken to the exercise pen or to be groomed (an hour before showing) in an area designated for handlers to set up their crates and grooming tables. At an unbenched show your car may serve as a bench for your dog.

To become a champion your dog must win fifteen points in competition with other dogs; a portion of the fifteen points must be awarded as major point wins (three to five points) under different judges.

HOW TO ENTER

If your dog is purebred and registered with the AKC — or eligible for registration — you may enter him in the appropriate show class for which his age, sex, and previous show record qualify him. You will find coming shows listed in the different dog magazines or at your petshop. Write to the secretary of the show, asking for the premium list. When you receive the entry form, fill it in carefully and send it back with the required entry fee. Then, before the show, you should receive your exhibitor's pass, which will admit you and your dog to the show. Here are the five official show classes:

PUPPY CLASS: Open to dogs at least six months and not more than twelve months of age. Limited to dogs whelped in the United States and Canada.

NOVICE CLASS: Open to dogs six months of age or older that have never won a first prize in any class other than the puppy class, and less than three first prizes in the novice class itself. Limited to dogs whelped in the United States or Canada.

BRED BY EXHIBITOR CLASS: Open to all dogs, except champions, six months of age or over which are exhibited by the same person, or his immediate family, or kennel that was the recognized breeder on the records of the American Kennel Club.

AMERICAN-BRED CLASS: Open to dogs that are not champions, six months of age or over, whelped in the United States after a mating which took place in the United States.

OPEN CLASS: Open to dogs six months of age or over, with no exceptions.

In addition there are local classes, the Specials Only class, and brace and team entries.

For full information on dog shows, read the book *HOW TO SHOW YOUR OWN DOG,* by Virginia Tuck Nichols. (T.F.H.)

ADVANCED PREPARATION

Before you go to a show your dog should be trained to gait at a trot beside you, with head up and in a straight line. In the ring you will have to gait your dog around the edge with other dogs and then individually up and down the center runner. In addition the dog must stand for examination by the judge, who will look at him closely and feel his head and body structure. He should be taught to stand squarely, hind feet slightly back, head up on the alert. Showing requires practice training sessions in advance. Get a friend to act as judge and set the dog up and "show" him a few minutes every day.

Sometime before the show, give your dog a bath so he will look his best. Get together all the things you will need to take to the show. You will want to take a water dish and a bottle of water for your dog (so he won't be affected by a change in drinking water). Take your show lead, bench chain (if it is a benched show), combs and brush, and the identification ticket sent by the show superintendent, noting the time you must be there and the place where the show will be held, as well as the time of judging.

THE DAY OF THE SHOW

Don't feed your dog the morning of the show, or give him at most a light meal. He will be more comfortable in the car on the way, and will show more enthusiastically. When you arrive at the show grounds, find out where he is to be benched and settle him there. Your bench or stall number is on your identification ticket, and the breed name will be on placards fastened to the ends of the row of benches. Once you have your dog securely fastened to his stall by a bench chain (use a bench crate instead of a chain if you prefer), locate the ring where your dog will be judged (the number and time of showing will be on the program of judging which came with your ticket). After this you may want to take your dog to the exercise ring to relieve himself, and give him a small drink of water. Your dog will have been groomed before the show, but give him a final brushing just before going into the show ring. When your breed judging is called, it is your responsibility to be at the ringside ready to go in. The steward will give you an armband which has on it the number of your dog.

Then, as you step into the ring, try to keep your knees from knocking! Concentrate on your dog and before you realize it you'll be out again, perhaps back with the winners of each class for more judging and finally, with luck, it will be over and you'll have a ribbon and trophy — and, of course, the most wonderful dog in the world.

BIBLIOGRAPHY

PS-606 DOLLARS IN DOGS, by Leon F. Whitney, D.V.M. The 26 chapters of this beautifully useful book tell you—frankly and clearly—how you can make money in the dog field. Every avenue to profit through dogs is explored thoroughly by Dr. Whitney, famous veterinarian and breeder. There are no punches pulled in the discussions of money-making opportunities available to everyone who wants to profit through his connection with canines. A real career-builder, 254 pages of solid and practical information, illustrated.
ISBN #0-87666-290-4
8½ x 5½ 255 pages 60 black & white photos

PS-684 DOG HOROSCOPE—YOUR DOG NEEDS A BIRTH-DAY. Probably the most clever and entertaining dog book ever published. Illustrated in color, readers are in for 64 pages of informative amusement, and you don't have to be an astrology fan to enjoy it.
ISBN #0-87666-317-X
8 x 5½ 64 pages 14 line illustrations

PS-607 HOW TO SHOW YOUR OWN DOG, by Virginia Tuck Nichols, paves the highroad to success in the fascinating and steadily growing avocation of exhibiting dogs. All of the intricacies of the show ring are explained in detail, coupled with wonderfully explicit treatments of the basics of dog shows; terms and definitions, how a champion is made, getting ready for the show, AKC rules and regulations, etc. Plus a bonus chapter on the tricks of the trade. In all, 254 well-illustrated pages that make winning in the dog show ring easier and a lot more fun.
ISBN #0-87666-390-0
8 ½ x 5½ 254 pages 136 black & white photos 10 line illustrations

H-925 DOG BREEDERS' HANDBOOK, by Ernest H. Hart. Here is the most complete and authoritative book on breeding ever written. In layman's language it clarifies all areas of this very necessary but often misunderstood subject. Beautifully presented and authored by a professional writer and recognized dog authority, the written word is augmented by profuse and pertinent illustrations.
ISBN #0-87666-286-6
85 black & white photos 12 line illustrations

PS-644 HOW TO TRAIN YOUR DOG, by Ernest H. Hart. Any dog is a better dog when well-trained. With the help of this book, any owner can do a first class job of training his dog. Fully and completely illustrated, the author takes you step by advancing step through the various areas of training. Many vital new concepts of training are advanced and discussed in this invaluable book. Color and black and white illustrations.
ISBN #0-87666-284-X
8½ x 5½ 107 pages 95 black & white photos 31 color photos

H-934 DOG OWNER'S ENCYCLOPEDIA OF VETERINARY MEDICINE, by Dr. Allan Hart. Here is a book that will become, next to his pet itself, the truest friend a dog-owner has. Page after page and chapter after chapter of valuable, pertinent information that allows an owner to make sure that his pet is given the best of care at all times. Easy to read yet brilliantly informative, this big book is a must.
ISBN #0-87666-287-4
8 x 5½ 186 pages 61 black & white photos 25 line illustrations